A WASHINGTON MONTHLY BOOK

The Hazards of Walking

*and Other Memos
from Your Bureaucrats*

Edited by Carol Trueblood
and Donna Fenn

Introduction by Charles Peters

HOUGHTON MIFFLIN COMPANY BOSTON 1982

Library of Congress Cataloging in Publication Data

Main entry under title:

The Hazards of walking and other memos from your bureaucrats.

    "Collection of . . . published and unpublished documents leaked to the Washington monthly's 'Memo of the month' department"—
    "A Washington monthly book."
    1. Government correspondence. 2. Memorandums. 3. Bureaucracy—United States. I. Trueblood, Carol. II. Fenn, Donna.
JK468.C75H39   081   82-3138
ISBN 0-395-32592-7 (pbk.)   AACR2

Printed in the United States of America.

v 10 9 8 7 6 5 4 3 2 1

Introduction

by Charles Peters

Francis Fisher, in an article called "The Art of the Memorandum" that appeared in one of the first issues of *The Washington Monthly*, wrote: "When I entered government, I assumed a memorandum was an official document that bureaucrat A writes to bureaucrat B when A wants B to do something. This was naive. B's usual response is to do nothing."

It may be that B is too busy writing his own memoranda. It is also possible—even probable—that A does not want B to do anything. He may write the memo simply because he wants to seem busy—and indeed the memo, once written, is proof that he was busy. Or his purpose may be, as an apt if inelegant expression puts it, to cover his ass.

There is good reason for the bureaucrat to prefer the appearance of action to action itself. Government agencies are established to deal with problems—the farm problem or the energy problem, for example. Solve the problem and the agency's reason for being is eliminated, along with (and here is where the true gravity of the matter becomes clear) the jobs of all its employees. It is understandable, then, that somewhere in the back of every bureaucrat's mind there is a yellow caution light that never stops blinking its warning of the perils of effective action. So even if the memo appears to recommend action, it will be "appropriate" action, and what is appropriate will never be defined. "When in doubt, mumble" is one of the fundamental principles of bureaucracy. This kind of memo is mumbling in print.

The self-defense memo, on the other hand, is often written with great clarity, for the author is seeking to make a record that will immunize him from attack by his rivals or by critics in the press, the Congress, the Office of Management and Budget, and the White House. The point at which such record making becomes more important than taking action is a crucial event in the life of an organization. In the organization's early days, the chemistry of new people and a new mission creates an atmosphere of vitality and urgency. Communication is by telephone or by hurried conversation in the halls. Gradually the excitement fades. People begin to worry more about their own careers than about their agency's purpose. At that precise moment they begin to write memos.

Most large American organizations seem to have arrived at that point. Since *The Washington Monthly* began publishing the Memo of the Month in 1969, readers have sent us memos from corporations, law firms, foundations, labor unions, and universities, as well as from government agencies at the federal, state, and local levels. This is, I think, not an insignificant fact. For I suspect that one of the main causes of our national decline has been the bureaucratization of America, to which these memos so fatuously attest.

Our primary purpose in assembling this collection is to amuse you, but we also hope that you will ponder the meaning of a culture whose primary form of written expression begins

To: . . . .

From: . . . .

Subject: . . . .

Neither snow, nor rain, nor heat, nor gloom of night stays these bureaucrats...

BEFORE THE
POSTAL RATE COMMISSION
WASHINGTON, D.C. 20268

POSTAL RATE AND FEE CHANGES, 1980 :

:   Docket No. R80-1

:

NOTICE TO ALL PARTIES

On April 9, 1981, the Postal Service filed its Brief on Reconsideration to the Commission. We stated therein our understanding that copies had been served on all parties to this docket.

We discovered at noon on April 14 that because of a back-up in the mail room, no copies of our Brief had as yet been mailed out. We regret this failure very much.

Respectfully submitted,

UNITED STATES POSTAL SERVICE

By its attorney:

Frances G. Beck
Assistant General Counsel

475 L'Enfant Plaza West, S.W.
Washington, D.C. 20260
April 15, 1981

UNITED STATES POSTAL SERVICE

DATE: August 3, 1981

OUR REF: G10:GFM:jcf

SUBJECT: Air Travel

TO:

Executive Committee Members
Regional Postmasters General

In view of the air controllers strike, no one is to travel
by air unless it is absolutely essential!

The Postmaster General, DPMG, SAPMGs and RPMGs will decide
what travel is essential. The limited flights which will
be available should not be used by people who do not have
urgent business to conduct.

If necessary, resort to conference calls and the mails to
communicate.

Gerald F. Merna
Executive Assistant to
   the Postmaster General

cc: Mr. Bolger
     Mr. Benson

MEMORANDUM

THE WHITE HOUSE
WASHINGTON

May 26, 1969

MEMORANDUM FOR: COLONEL HUGHES

The President would like to have the bowling ball man come
in and fit Mrs. Nixon and Tricia for balls as soon as possible.
Could arrangements be made for this immediately, please.

H. R. HALDEMAN

cc:
Mr. Chapin

MEMORANDUM

DEPARTMENT OF HEALTH AND HUMAN SERVICES
PUBLIC HEALTH SERVICE
NATIONAL INSTITUTES OF HEALTH
NATIONAL INSTITUTE OF ENVIRONMENTAL HEALTH SCIENCES

TO : Administrative Officers
Timekeepers

DATE: December 23, 1981

FROM : Executive Officer

SUBJECT: Holiday Greetings from the President Amendment #1

In my memorandum advising that President Reagan was permitting a half-day off on Thursday, December 24, 1981, I advised that this was to be treated as a holiday for pay and leave purposes. We have now been advised that it is not a holiday but is an administrative dismissal (excused absence).

Employees who would have been on approved leave Thursday afternoon will _not_ be charged leave.

Employees who cannot be spared and who work Thursday afternoon are not entitled to overtime or holiday pay for the normal afternoon work period.

Paul G. Waugaman

PRESIDENTIAL DETERMINATIONS

[Determination of August 5, 1975]

Eligibility of Fiji To Purchase Defense Articles and Defense Services Under the Foreign Military Sales Act, as Amended

[Presidential Determination No. 76–1]

Memorandum for the Secretary of State

THE WHITE HOUSE,
Washington, August 5, 1975.

Pursuant to the authority vested in me by Section 3(a)(1) of the Foreign Military Sales Act, as amended, I hereby find that the sale of defense articles and defense services to the Government of Fiji will strengthen the security of the United States and promote world peace.

You are directed on my behalf to report this finding to Congress.

This finding, which amends Presidential Determination No. 73–10 of January 2, 1973 (38 FR 7211), as amended by Presidential Determinations No. 73–12 of April 26, 1973 (38 FR 12799), No. 74–9 of December 13, 1973 (39 FR 3537), No. 75–2 of October 29, 1974 (39 FR 39863), and No. 75–21 of May 20, 1975 (40 FR 24889), shall be published in the FEDERAL REGISTER.

Gerald R. Ford

[FR Doc.75–22681 Filed 8–22–75;2:53 pm]

2976

THE WHITE HOUSE

WASHINGTON

January 22, 1979

MEMORANDUM FOR MEMBERS OF WHITE HOUSE STAFF

FROM: JERRY RAFSHOON *Jerry*

SUBJECT: State of the Union Address Talking Points

(It is important that the State of the Union speech be "sold
properly. It provides us with a good opportunity - at midterm -
to put the policies of the Administration and the President's
philosophy in a larger context. It directly addresses the
charge of "themelessness". We should not be defensive about
its theme or the fact that it is thematic.)

--It is an important speech - a summing up and a look forward
at mid term. It is Carter's speech. He has spent more time
on it than any other speech since becoming President. There
have been at least a half-dozen meetings and as many drafts -
each returned with extensive Presidential rewriting.

--The President made clear that it was to be a serious, thematic
speech providing the best context to date of his approach to
the Presidency, his view of the nation's problems, his vision
for the future. There are few applause lines - no boiler-plate
political rhetoric. The impact of the speech will come from
the ideas contained in it.

--The theme of the speech is that we must build a new foundation
for America's future. Specifically, we must restore the confidence of our people by building a foundation for a balanced,
stable economic growth; we must restore trust to the poltical
process by building a new foundation for competent and compas-
sionate government; we must maintain a stable peace in the world
by building a new foundation based on cooperation and diversity.
The speech is divided into three parts: the economy (confidence)
government (trust) and foreign affairs (peace). In each section
there is a brief review of the progress of the last two years
and a look ahead to the priority of 1979 and beyond.

Continued

--The theme is quintessential Carter. It is positive. It reflects his propensity for long-range planning. It is moderate. It is hopeful but realistic. There is nothing contrived about it. There was no effort to "find" a slogan. "New foundation" emerged from the process of developing the most definitive statement to date of the President's approach to his job.

(The "new foundation" theme will certainly be ridiculed to some extent by commentators and cartoonists. It is important that we not retreat from it so that six months from now people will say, "Remember that 'new foundation' thing Carter tried? Whatever happened to that?" The theme will hold up in the long run if we stick with it.)

Department of Energy
Portsmouth Area Office
P.O. Box 700
Piketon, Ohio 45661

January 30, 1981

All PAO Employees

TRIPPING HAZARDS

One of the ways to guard against it is to always put your best foot forward. It may have more to do with how other people perceive your ability to walk than your own perception.

Each of us should reflect for a moment on how we are perceived to be walking around about lunch time each day.

We should also advise our contractor employee associates regarding the use of Government vehicles in lieu of walking to some noontime functions. This practice also is somewhat hazardous.

Wilbur L. Walker
Area Manager

EP-66:WLW

DEPARTMENT OF THE ARMY
HEADQUARTERS PRESIDIO OF SAN FRANCISCO
PRESIDIO OF SAN FRANCISCO, CALIFORNIA 94129

REPLY TO ATTENTION OF:

AFZM-SAF   2 2 FEB 1977

SUBJECT: Safety Letter 1-77

SEE DISTRIBUTION

1. This safety letter should be discussed with all personnel and then posted on the unit bulletin board for 30 days.

2. The hazards of walking:

    a. The investigation of accidents involving walking and working surfaces reveals that most accidents are the direct result of inattention. Most of the incidents do not involve lost-time injuries but do result in pain and inconvenience.

    b. This inattention coupled with reading or reviewing documents while walking; going up or down stairs with both hands occupied (not holding the handrail); and wearing footwear of unusual design are responsible for the great majority of mishaps.

    c. The character, age and composition of walking surfaces are frequently cited as the culprit in mishaps, but objective investigation suggests that the preponderance of these mishaps are the fault of the individual.

    d. Tripping, slipping and falling accidents are not restricted to the work environment. Both adults and children are injured daily due to the same causes outside work areas. Awareness of the hazards as well as supervision of the children may help reduce the severity and frequency of these accidents.

3. Any mishap can result in injury to an individual's pride or person, and all mishaps result in some loss of productive time. Individual responsibility to oneself and others is a key element in the prevention of accidents. The constant awareness and application of this responsibility are an absolute necessity in order to efficiently accomplish the assigned mission at reduced costs and to improve the morale and welfare of the military/civilian community at the Presidio of San Francisco.

FOR THE COMMANDER:

FRANK   CHICAGO
OFF. ACC
Assistant Adjutant

DISTRIBUTION:
A - B - C
Plus:
SAF (1,500 cy)

GQ-73 (Rev. 1-65)

ILLINOIS DEPARTMENT OF LABOR
BUREAU OF EMPLOYMENT SECURITY

MEMORANDUM

Date: **April 30, 1971**

To: David Gassman   Office:
        Statistician II

From: Benjamin Greenstein, Chief   Office:
        Research and Statistics

Subject: Hazardous Use of Coffee Pot

The afternoon of April 29, while Mr. Arthur Haverly was on vacation, an
electric coffee pot was plugged in in his office and left unattended. It
spread noxious fumes through the office and scorched a table belonging to
the State.

You admitted that you plugged in that coffee pot and that you did it,
although Mr. Haverly had told you that I had requested that it should not
be done due to previous adverse experience. When I asked you why you
plugged in that coffee pot, although I had requested that it should not be
done, you stated that you did not take it that seriously.

I may note also that Mr. Haverly informed me the previous day that he had
not authorized you to connect the coffee pot in his office.

The following facts, therefore, emerge:

1. You had used your supervisor's office for cooking coffee without
   his authorization.

2. You did so, although you knew that I had requested that it should
   not be done.

3. You had left the coffee pot unattended. For that matter, there
   may have been a conflict between performing agency work and
   attending to the coffee pot.

4. You created a fire hazard for your fellow workers and subjected
   them to noxious fumes.

5. When I asked you why you plugged in the coffee pot in spite of my
   request to the contrary, you stated that you did not take it that
   seriously. This is a rejection of supervision.

6. Your disregard of my authority has resulted in discomfort to your
   fellow workers and damage to State property.

Continued

7. On April 30, the day following the above actions and conversation,
    at 8:25 in the morning, I noted that you had again plugged in the
    coffee pot. When I pointed out that you were aware that I had
    asked you not to plug it in, you replied that it is not 8:30 yet.
    I then told you that I am in charge of the section, even though it
    is not 8:30 yet.

What should be done with respect to your actions, as specified above, is
under consideration. In the meantime you are emphatically requested not
to repeat the hazard you created by plugging in the coffee pot.

BENJAMIN GREENSTEIN, Chief
Research and Statistics

PENTAGON BUILDING

CIRCULAR

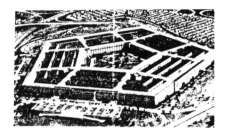

NO: 76-49   **DATE:**

19 November 1976

EXPIRATION:

31 December 1976

SUBJECT: Pentagon Building Vacuum Cleaner Operations

The Deputy Assistant Secretary of Defense (Environment and Safety) requested that the following information concerning the vacuum cleaner noise problem be disseminated to Pentagon Building occupants:

a. <u>Issue:</u> Numerous employee complaints indicate that vacuum cleaners operated by GSA Custodial Services' personnel emit sound levels which:

(1) Exceed permissible noise limits specified in occupational safety and health standards.

(2) Disrupt important daily activities.

b. <u>Facts:</u>

(1) Pentagon daytime (vice night) cleaning schedules are part of the energy conservation program.

(2) Vacuum cleaner sound level measurements were recorded as follows:

(a) Two machine types register 82-90 decibels.

(b) One type machine registers 92-96 decibels.

c. <u>Evaluation:</u> Occupational safety and health standards permit employee exposure to 90 decibels of sound for eight consecutive hours without the use of protective hearing devices. Pentagon occupants are not exposed to hazardous sound levels under existing standards. Operators of machines which register 92-96 decibels should use protective ear devices, and are required to do so.

NO: 76-50
SUBJECT: Pentagon Building Vacuum Cleaner Operations

Continued

    d. <u>Actions:</u> Although there is no violation of safety
and occupational health standards, the General Services Administration acknowledges the disruptive effect of the vacuum
operation during work hours. Accordingly:

        (1) Consideration is being given to revising vacuum
cleaner operator work schedules to the 4-8 p.m. time period
by 31 December 1976.

        (2) An effort is underway to obtain quieter vacuum
machines.

                            PAUL K. HASELBUSH
                            DOD Building Administrator
                            Pentagon

DISTRIBUTION: B (OSD) (DA) (DN) (DAF) (DIA) (DCA) (DCPA)

The Bureaucrat Gives Instructions

ADMINISTRATIVE MEMORANDUM

OFFICE OF THE LEGAL ADVISER

Number 5B
June 13, 1977

SUBJECT: Additional Responsibilities of the L Duty Officer

Effective immediately, in addition to the responsibilities listed in the earlier memoranda identifying the responsibilities of the L duty officer, upon arriving in the Office on Saturday mornings the duty officer should get a copy of the NEW YORK TIMES for the Legal Adviser's Office.

The following procedure should be used in order to get a copy of the NEW YORK TIMES:

Take the freight elevator closest to the Office of the Legal Adviser (next door to L/PM, Room 6429)down to the basement. Turn left through closed double doors and follow corridor to the left until you reach Room B-528. Ask the attendant for the Legal Adviser's copy of the NEW YORK TIMES.

If you have any difficulty in obtaining a copy of the NEW YORK TIMES following this procedure, inform L/EX of this fact the following Monday morning.

L C. KOLB, M.D.
COMMISSIONER

McKINLLY, M.D.
DEPUTY COMMISSIONER

GERALD F. DUNN
DEPUTY COMMISSIONER

STATE OF NEW YORK
DEPARTMENT OF MENTAL HYGIENE
DIVISION OF ADMINISTRATION
44 HOLLAND AVENUE
ALBANY, N. Y. 12229

February 17, 1978

DIVISION OF ADMINISTRATION
NUTRITION BULLETIN NO. 78-06

TO: Facility Directors, Deputy Director for Administration
        Business Officer, Institution Food Administrator, Dietitian

        Central Office: Food Service Distribution List

FROM: Jack J. Bellick, R.D.
        Director
        Bureau of Nutrition Services

SUBJECT: Fork Splitting of Supply Support English Muffin Buns (W054240)

In order to preserve the natural wholesomeness and flavor of english muffins, it was necessary to distribute them to you uncut. Since the type of cut (forked vs. sliced) significantly affects the flavor and texture of the toasted product, we recommend the fork cut which provides the "peaks and valleys" symmetry necessary for maximum flavor and texture.

The attached picture of an eighteen pronged cutter with plastic handle (see attached picture given actual size) will greatly speed up the task of fork cutting these muffin buns as opposed to using a standard table fork. Although the cutter was originally designed and sold as an onion holder (for thin slicing), it is particularly effective as an "English Muffin Bun Splitter." This cutter can be purchased at your local hardware or department store. We urge that you instruct your staff in the right use of this cutter.

I. Breakfast or Snack Use
    Method: 1) Insert the splitter into the side of the muffin.
          2) Rotate the muffin in a 90° turn and insert the splitter into the side so that the second cut is perpendicular to the first cut.

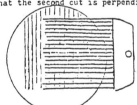

          3) Pry open the muffin. Toast in rotary toaster (preferred) or pop-up toaster.

          4) Spread with butter or margarine and serve.

II. Breakfast or Luncheon Use
    Method: 1) Slice with serrated edge knife.

          2) Use as a bun for "Egg McMuffin" or use as a base for individual "miniature English Pizzas."

Should you devise a more efficient method of producing the same results, we would appreciate hearing from you so as we can share your idea with other facilities.

STATE OF ARKANSAS
Bill Clinton, Governor

DEPARTMENT OF HUMAN SERVICES
Gail S. Huecker, Director

DIVISION OF MENTAL RETARDATION-
DEVELOPMENTAL DISABILITIES SERVICES
Dr. Joseph P. Cozzolino, Commissioner

Suite 400, Waldon Building	7th & Main Streets	Little Rock, Arkansas 72201	501/371-2333

MEMORANDUM

TO: Mr. Fred Cheyunski, Administrator, EPMS
Mr. Charles Elliott, Deputy Commissioner, Community Services
Ms. Henrietta Jenkins, Deputy Commissioner, CP & RS
Dr. Ada Thompson, Deputy Commissioner, Professional Support Services
Mr. Ron Weis, Deputy Commissioner, Institutional Services

FROM: Dr. Harold Nethercutt
Deputy Commissioner
Administrative Services

DATE: April 22, 1980

SUBJECT: Daylight-Saving Time

Daylight-Saving Time begins this year at 2:00 a.m., Sunday, April 27. Clocks should be set forward one hour.

Harold Nethercutt, Ed.D.
Deputy Commissioner

HN:mm

cc: Dr. Joseph Cozzolino, Commissioner, MR-DDS
Mr. Tony Zingarelli, Assistant Commissioner
Mr. Howard Watson, Director, DHS Public Affairs
Mr. Dennis Bonge, Accounting Manager, MR-DDS
Mr. Sam Fleming, Reimbursement Officer, MR-DDS
Mr. Don Fugett, Data Processing Manager, MR-DDS
Mr. Jim Hickman, Purchasing Manager, MR-DDS
Mrs. Gene Ockerman, Personnel Manager, MR-DDS
Mr. Bill Porter, Inventory Control Manager, MR-DDS
Mrs. Theda Carroll, Management Project Analyst
Mrs. Alice Johnson, Administrative Assistant
Mr. Louis Brown, Superintendent, Booneville Unit
Dr. Russ Burbank, Superintendent, Arkadelphia/Conway Unit
Mr. Maurice Caldwell, Superintendent, SEAHDC, Warren
Mr. Samuel DeMarco, Superintendent, Alexander Unit
Mr. Thomas Lewins, Superintendent, Jonesboro Unit
Mr. Ray Biggerstaff, Business Manager, Alexander Unit
Mr. Mike Cowart, Business Manager, Arkadelphia Unit
Mr. Bill Hoggard, Business Manager, Conway Unit
Mr. Al Peer, Business Manager, SEAHDC, Warren
Mr. Larry Wells, Business Manager, Booneville Unit
Mr. Bill Wood, Business Manager, Jonesboro Unit

MICHIGAN
HOUSE OF REPRESENTATIVES
LANSING, MICHIGAN 48909

MEMORANDUM

TO: Josephine Martin

FROM: Doug Drake

DATE: October 4, 1978

SUBJECT: Sign-out procedures.

Josephine, I've noticed that you did not sign out when you left
the building yesterday to attend mass (Tom Husband, Mary Kay and
I were standing in the parking lot and saw you enter the church).

The procedure is:

    Sign out, with a desination, phone number and approximate
    time of return, whenever you leave your office.

DCD:slh

Fremont Union High School District

589 WEST FREMONT AVENUE
SUNNYVALE, CALIFORNIA 94087
(408) 735-6060

●

JACK ROPER
SUPERINTENDENT OF SCHOOLS

HIGH SCHOOLS
ADULT/COMMUNITY
BLANEY
CUPERTINO
FREMONT
HOMESTEAD
LYNBROOK
MONTA VISTA
SUNNYVALE

DAILY ROUTINE PROCEDURES

1. Remove items from top of desk carefully, dust thoroughly, and replace items.

2. Sharpen pencils morning and afternoon. Be sure at least two of them are red pencils. Number 3 hard lead preferred.

3. Wash ashtrays each morning, empty throughout the day at convenient intervals when office is not in use.

4. Update all calendars on a DAILY basis, particularly pocket calendar. Ask for pocket calendar DAILY.

5. Before leaving each day, check with supervisor to see if there are immediate needs or special instructions for the next day.

6. Before leaving each day, leave clearly marked listing of appointments including telephone number of visitor and subject of appointment and any related file materials attached to the listing and place all in a prominent place on my desk:

   Be certain to provide all possible background material for appointments and meetings and eliminate confusion by clearly marking to which item each set of material pertains.

7. Be sure to call to my attention any appointments scheduled prior to 7:45 a.m. or after 4:30 p.m. Please do this the day BEFORE such appointments at least. If I am not available, please leave me note with materials for the next day.

8. For all meetings which are by invitation, save invitation and put in the file for the meeting.

9. When you are going to be out of the office or late, you are to report to me or in my absence to Warren Bryld. Adrian Stanga is in charge when I am absent.

10. Please serve Sanka (without cream or sugar) to me upon my arrival each morning. Anytime guests are present, offer and serve coffee or tea. Be in charge of supplies and clean-up for the office coffee service.

Continued

Fremont Union High School District

589 WEST FREMONT AVENUE
SUNNYVALE, CALIFORNIA 94087
(408) 735-6060

●

JACK ROPER
SUPERINTENDENT OF SCHOOLS

HIGH SCHOOLS
ADULT/COMMUNITY
BLANEY
CUPERTINO
FREMONT
HOMESTEAD
LYNBROOK
MONTA VISTA
SUNNYVALE

TELEPHONE PROCEDURE

1. In a pleasant voice and manner, ascertain name of caller, his company or school affiliation, and nature of call.

2. Do not indicate whether or not I am in the office.

3. If I am in conference, state that. Then ask in a pleasant way if someone else may be of assistance. Then give me a note letting me know who called and to whom caller was referred.

4. If I am in the office, I will take all calls from members of the Board of Trustees and members of the Administrative Council. If not, again, try in pleasant way to ascertain nature of call and refer it to someone else if possible. Again, give me note letting me know who called and to whom call was referred.

5. Take complete written message and write on message form. Place on dial of my telephone so I can see immediately upon my return to the desk that someone has called.

   Check with me near end of the day for reminders of calls I have been unable to return and assist me in return of calls.

   If I do not return to the office to receive a message, you please return call and let caller know I will try to return call the following day.

6. Try not to let phone ring more than three rings. Hopefully, it can be answered by the third ring.

7. If you are away from your desk, please arrange for telephone coverage. Also, before you leave the desk, please let me know that you will be away.

(Plus three more pages)

OFFICE OF THE SECRETARY OF THE TREASURY

WASHINGTON, D.C. 20220

April 8, 1981

MEMORANDUM FOR UNDER SECRETARIES
ASSISTANT SECRETARIES

Subject: Briefing Books for the Secretary

All briefing books prepared for Secretary Regan should be assembled in soft/flexible covered binders. The Secretary prefers not to have hard cover binders sent to him.

If for a particular meeting books are required for several individuals, only the Secretary's binder need be soft cover. Other meeting participants may use hard covered binders.

Steven L. Skancke
Acting Executive Secretary

From the Deputy Assistant
Associate Administrator. . .

UNITED STATES ENVIRONMENTAL PROTECTION AGENCY
WASHINGTON, D.C. 20460

SEP 2 4 1981

MEMORANDUM FOR   Associate Administrators
                 Assistant Administrators
                 Office Directors
                 Regional Administrators

    We have had some confusion as to the designations
A/O and O/A. To avoid further conflicts, A/O will
mean the Office of the Administrator and O/A will be
Office of Administration.

John E. Daniel
Chief of Staff

FEDERAL ENERGY ADMINISTRATION
WASHINGTON, D.C. 20461

APR 14 1975

OFFICE OF THE ASSISTANT ADMINISTRATOR

MEMORANDUM FOR: FEA Senior Staff

SUBJECT: Executive Position Titles

In the past few weeks the number of titles available to important FEA personnel has been drastically reduced. It is also understood that OMB will shortly place a freeze on the proliferation of FEA titles. In the interest of maintaining staff morale, it has been decided to make the remaining titles available on a limited basis for the next two weeks. Written requests and justifications for the remaining titles should be filed with the Deputy Associate Assistant Administrator for Management Nomenclature, telephone number, 961-8534.

Those titles currently in use are:

1. Administrator
2. Deputy Administrator
3. Assistant Administrator
4. Deputy Assistant Administrator
5. Associate Deputy Administrator
6. Associate Assistant Administrator
7. Deputy Associate Assistant Administrator *

Those titles available for selection during the next two weeks are:

1. Associate Administrator
2. Deputy Associate Administrator
3. Assistant Associate Administrator
4. Deputy Assistant Associate Administrator
5. Assistant Deputy Associate Administrator
6. Assistant Deputy Administrator
7. Assistant Associate Deputy Administrator
8. Associate Assistant Deputy Administrator
9. Associate Deputy Assistant Administrator

---

* Some offices have opted to call their Deputy Associate Assistant Administrators Office Directors. These persons, of course, are free to use the more formal title, Deputy Associate Assistant Administrator.

Although other titles are available, such as Deputy Associate Deputy Administrator, good form dictates avoidance of such redundancy. It is hoped that all desirous of titles will be satisfied with those listed above.

Continued

A memorandum describing titles available to the Office of
General Counsel, Office of Congressional Affairs, Office of
Communications and Public Affairs, Office of Private Grievances
and Redress, and Office of Intergovernmental and Special Programs
will be circulated within the next two weeks. The use of informal
titles, such as Executive or Special Assistant, will remain
flexible as in the past.

Leonard B. Pouliot
Assistant Administrator
Management and Administration

THE SECRETARY OF HEALTH AND HUMAN SERVICES
WASHINGTON, D.C. 20201

JUN 2 2 1981

MEMORANDUM FOR: See Below

SUBJECT: Organizational Nomenclature

I have decided to change the term which we in the Department use to refer to the Public Health Service (PHS), the Social Security Administration (SSA), the Health Care Financing Administration (HCFA), and the Office of Human Development Services (OHDS) from "Principal Operating Component" to "Operating Division." Effective immediately, please use only the term Operating Division when referring to PHS, SSA, HCFA, or OHDS. The appropriate abbreviation for the term Operating Division is "OPDIV."

The Office of the Secretary (OS) contains staff divisions ("STAFFDIV"), rather than operating divisions. When referring to all of the staff divisions (ASL, ASMB, ASPA, ASPE, ASPER, GC, IG, IOS, OCR) in OS collectively, use the term "OS Staff Divisions."

To minimize the costs associated with changing terminology, please replace "POC" with "OPDIV" as you reissue documents, manuals, etc., for other reasons. Do not make special revisions to existing documents only to change the "POC" terminology.

Richard S. Schweiker
Secretary

INTERDEPARTMENTAL

June 19, 1981

TO: Gerard Hogan, Library Supervisor I
                Library
                FM-25

FROM: Laurie T. Wold, Personnel Representative
                Staff Personnel
                JA-10

SUBJECT: Reallocation

The Higher Education Personnel Board abolished the Library Supervisor I classification and created a new classification, Library Supervisor A, effective July 1, 1981. The assigned salary range, range 22, remains unchanged.

Accordingly, your position has been reallocated to Library Supervisor A effective July 1, 1981. There is no change in your salary.

Please note that you may, if you so elect, appeal this decision per WAC 251-06-070 by writing the Director of the Higher Education Personnel Board within thirty calendar days of the effective date of the action.

LTW/dm

cc: Charles Chamberlin
     Budget Office

DICKSTEIN, SHAPIRO & MORIN

ARE PLEASED TO ANNOUNCE THAT

HELEN R. KANOVSKY

FORMERLY SPECIAL ASSISTANT TO THE SECRETARY,

EXECUTIVE ASSISTANT TO THE UNDER SECRETARY

AND ASSOCIATE EXECUTIVE SECRETARY,

DEPARTMENT OF HEALTH AND HUMAN SERVICES

AND PREVIOUSLY

SPECIAL ASSISTANT TO THE SECRETARY,

DEPARTMENT OF HOUSING AND URBAN DEVELOPMENT

HAS RETURNED TO THE FIRM

2101 L STREET, N. W.   598 MADISON AVENUE
WASHINGTON. D. C. 20037   NEW YORK, N. Y. 10022

FEBRUARY 1, 1981

Advisory Council on
Historic Preservation
1522 K Street N.W.
Washington, D.C. 20005

January 11, 1977

Memorandum

To: Council Staff

From: Executive Director

Subject: Correspondence

In all correspondence requiring the use of the name of the Council, the
full name Advisory Council on Historic Preservation should be used when
the name first appears. Thereafter, the Council should be used never
the Advisory Council. This same pattern should be used in oral or
written presentations. Our objective is to subordinate the term
Advisory. At the December meeting, it was suggested by several members
that the Council's name be changed by deleting the term Advisory. This
may become a Council legislative initiative. Until that time, the word
should be used only when necessary.

May 1, 1974

DEANS, DIRECTORS, DEPARTMENT CHAIRMEN

RE: Use of Affirmative Action in titles

Because affirmative action is becoming so popular in all phases of operations, more people are beginning to use affirmative action as working titles and as divisions within their offices. It is becoming increasingly difficult to distinguish persons in various offices employing the same or similar titles using the words "affirmative action". Therefore, as referenced in the PPM 250-200 and 230-6, I would like to reiterate that Dr. Paul Saltman maintains the title of Academic Affirmative Action Coordinator; Mr. Bernard Sisco, the title of Staff Affirmative Action Coordinator; and Mr. Jack Douglass, the title of Affirmative Action Monitor. Mr. Douglass still maintains the only Affirmative Action Office, per se, as both academic and staff coordinators operate out of the academic and staff personnel offices. For clarification purposes, we will list these three offices in the next campus directory under affirmative action.

I should like to request that even though we operate affirmatively out of several offices, that persons handling affirmative action apart from the above, use the title of Departmental Affirmative Action Advisor; in this way there will be no confusion as to who is the Affirmative Action Coordinator or which offices are the campus affirmative action offices.

W. D. McElroy
Chancellor

DEPARTMENT OF THE AIR FORCE
HEADQUARTERS AIR FORCE LOGISTICS COMMAND
WRIGHT-PATTERSON AIR FORCE BASE, OHIO 45433

REPLY TO
ATTN OF   MMWC

SUBJECT: SAC/Plattsburg C/R B3264-0140/C3271-1630/D3289-3687, FSN 8820-
188-3880, Dog Patrol, Explosive (Your ltr, 17 Oct 73)

TO: WRAMA/MMSEB

1. Recommend clarification of the Plattsburg request, the
FSNs used, WRAMA's comments, and FSNs in the TA.

2. There will be a tendency towards confusion unless more
or more explicit information is given. AFLC cannot identify
any FSN to Dog Detection - Explosive or as WRAMA puts it in
17 Oct 73 letter, Patrol Dog/Explosive. We cannot determine
whether they want a dog or an explosive. TA 538 lists
FSN 8820-435-9005 as a Dog-Patrol which may be an animal to
ferret out narcotics or explosives.

3. Plattsburg started out with a request for FSN 8820-243-
7542 which is related to narcotics (a/w 538C) not explosives.
The FSN was supplanted with 8820-188-<u>3880</u>. TA 538 and TA 002
list 8820-128-<u>2880</u>. Was there an error? Is 188-3880 a new
number? Is 188-3880 a dog to sniff out explosives? Also
what does Plattsburg really want: Dog-Explosive or Dog-
Narcotics? Why has an exchange been offered in your 17 Oct
letter?

4. Please review this whole thing for AFLC. Clarification
is in order and a change to TA 538 for better identification
seems in order.

FOR THE COMMANDER

CHARLES K. PICKELL
Aerospace Equipment Division
Office of DCS/Materiel Management

DEPARTMENT OF THE ARMY
HEADQUARTERS, PICATINNY ARSENAL
DOVER, NEW JERSEY 07801

SARPA-CP

25 Jan 74

Mr. Jay A. Berger
100 Center Grove Rd/
Apt 8-14
Randolph, NJ 07801

Dear Mr. Berger:

Your Suggestion No.   H34-74   Subject: Removal of silver tip on
Retractable Ball-Point Pens
which was referred to primary interested agencies for evaluation, was not
recommended for adoption. Reasons for this decision by the evaluator(s)
are given in the attached comments.

Although your suggestion was not given favorable consideration, the
interest and initiative you displayed in submitting it are appreciated.

Ideas received through the Army Suggestion Plan have resulted in benefits
of many millions of dollars to the government, improvement in morale and
elimination of numerous safety hazards.

You are urged to continue your participation in the Army Suggestion Plan.
Let your ideas be for Economy - Safety - Progress.

Sincerely yours,

1 Incl
Evaluation

for Incentive Awards Administrator

SUGGESTION EVALUATION

For use of this form, see CPPM 1, Sec 12; the proponent agency is Office of the Deputy Chief of Staff for Personnel.

TO: (Include ZIP Code)	FROM: (Include ZIP Code)
Incentive Awards Administrator SMUPA-CP, Bldg 118	Acting Chief, Station Supply & Stock Control Division, Bldg 91

1. SUGGESTION TITLE	2. SUGGESTION NUMBER
Removal of Silver Tip on Retractable Ball-Point Pens	H-34-74

3.   ACTION TAKEN OR RECOMMENDED

a. APPROVED FOR ADOPTION.   ☐ TOTALLY   ☐ PARTIALLY OR WITH MODIFICATION (Explain in Item 4.)

DATE SUGGESTION WAS OR WILL BE PUT INTO EFFECT   ☐ ALSO RECOMMEND CONSIDERATION FOR WIDER APPLICATION AS INDICATED IN ITEM 4.

b. ALREADY IN USE OR UNDER CONSIDERATION. (Explain in Item 4 indicating whether this suggestion contributed to the action in any way.)

c. RECOMMEND ADOPTION, BUT APPROVAL NOT WITHIN JURISDICTION OF THIS OFFICE. REASONS FOR RECOMMENDATION ARE CONTAINED IN ITEM 4.

XX d. NOT RECOMMENDED FOR ADOPTION FOR REASONS SHOWN IN ITEM 4.

e. OTHER (Specify in Item 4)

4. REASONS FOR ACTION TAKEN OR RECOMMENDED (If more space is needed, continue on reverse)

This suggestion is not recommended for adoption in accordance with
inclosed evaluation by General Services Administration.

DEPARTMENT OF THE ARMY
THE ADJUTANT GENERAL CENTER
WASHINGTON, D.C. 20314

DAAG-AMO-P

10 January 1974

SUBJECT: Suggestion, Removal of Silver Tip on Retractable Ball-Point Pens,
H-34-74

Commander
Picatinny Arsenal
ATTN: SARPA-IS-SS-Sm
Dover, New Jersey 07801

Subject suggestion is returned not recommended for adoption. General
Service Administration comments are attached.

FOR THE COMMANDER:

1 Incl
as

J. R. ROBINSON, JR
MAJ, AGC
Chief, Operations Division

UNITED STATES OF AMERICA
GENERAL SERVICES ADMINISTRATION

Office of Administration
Washington, D.C. 20405

DATE 12-13-73

REPLY TO ATTN OF: BPOR

SUBJECT: Suggestion No. *H-34-74*

Mrs. Marie Lee (IDR)
Adjutant General Center
Department of the Army
ATTN: DAAG-ASO-P
Room GA159, Forrestal Bldg.
Washington, DC 20314

We are returning an employee suggestion which was forwarded to General Services Administration for evaluation.

The suggestion has been evaluated and has not been recommended for adoption. The reasons are given in the enclosed evaluation.

Although the suggestion was not recommended for adoption, we appreciate the time and thought the suggestor has given this suggestion.

FRANCIS E. CAMMARATA
Central Office Suggestion Coordinator

Enclosures
Our File No. **OA 74-127**

Suggestion No: OA 74-127
Date Referred: 10/31/73

EVALUATION

The suggester alleges that the metal plunger and metal band are not needed and should be eliminated thereby saving material and money.

The ball point pens are designed to be serviceable during the life of several refills. The metal parts are intended to improve the performance, serviceability and aesthetic value of the pens.

Prior to revision of GG-B-0060C, the Government received numerous complaints about the quality of the pens. Revision "C" of subject specification was developed and issued after extensive consultation with industry and Federal agencies. From the response, it appears that the majority of the users are now satisfied with the design, quality, aesthetic value, and cost of the pens.

This office is aware of the apparent savings that could be realized by redesigning and changing some of the requirements of the pens. We are in contact with industry and have initiated a testing project with the intent of finding ways of improving the quality of the pens and reducing cost. After further study, we will implement those changes that will decrease the cost of the pens, provided these changes will not impair the quality and aesthetic value of the pens. Future changes cannot be attributed to this or previous suggestions.

Adoption of this suggestion is not recommended.

DEFENSE LOGISTICS AGENCY
HEADQUARTERS
CAMERON STATION
ALEXANDRIA, VIRGINIA 22314

IN REPLY
REFER TO DLSSO

18 NOV 1981

MEMORANDUM FOR ASSISTANT SECRETARIES OF DEFENSE
       ASSISTANTS TO THE SECRETARY OF DEFENSE
       CHAIRMAN, JOINT CHIEFS OF STAFF
       SECRETARIES OF THE MILITARY DEPARTMENTS
       DIRECTORS OF THE DEFENSE AGENCIES
       COMMANDANT, U.S. COAST GUARD
       ADMINISTRATOR, GENERAL SERVICES ADMINISTRATION

SUBJECT: Introduction of New Title, DLSSO

The DoD Military Standard Logistics Systems Office (DoD MILSO), the DoD Logistics Data Element Standardization and Management Office (DoD LOGDESMO) and the Defense Automatic Addressing System Office (DAASO) were assigned to the DoD Military Standard Logistics Systems and Data Element Standardization and Management Office (DoD MILSDESMO) on 4 February 1979, as approved by the Deputy Assistant Secretary of Defense (Supply, Maintenance and Services) (DASD(SM&S)) memorandum of 16 May 1978, subject: Transfer of the Logistics Data Element Standardization and Management Office. As described in DoD Directives 4000.25 and 5000.27, the DoD MILSO, DoD LOGDESMO and DAASO are mutually supporting and essential elements in accomplishing common DoD policies and objectives for achieving standardization, compatibility and interface relationships for DoD logistics systems.

On 8 May 1981 the Deputy Assistant Secretary of Defense (SM&T), authorized the title of DoD MILSDESMO to be shortened to "Defense Logistics Standard Systems Office (DLSSO)." DoD MILSO, DoD LOGDESMO and DAASO will continue to be identified as separate offices under the DLSSO. The Chief, DLSSO, will continue to receive policy guidance from the Assistant Secretary of Defense, Manpower, Reserve Affairs and Logistics (ASD(MRA&L)) and Assistant Secretary of Defense (Comptroller) (ASD(C)) while administratively reporting to the Director through the Assistant Director, Plans, Policies and Programs, Defense Logistics Agency. The Chief, DLSSO, has been directed to use the distinctive letterhead at Enclosure 1 to clearly distinguish the DLSSO as an OSD operation.

FOR THE DIRECTOR:

M. ROGER PETERSON
Major General, USAF
Assistant Director,
Plans, Policies and Programs

1 Encl

DISPOSITION FORM

For use of this form, see AR 340-15; the proponent agency is The Adjutant General's Office.

REFERENCE OR OFFICE SYMBOL	SUBJECT
ATZI-CS	October Commander's Call

TO	SEE DISTRIBUTION	FROM	Chief of Staff, ADMINCEN	DATE	5 October 1976	CMT 1

1. The October Commander's Call will be held at 1530, 20 October 1976, in the Ballroom, FBH Officers' Club. The guest speaker will be Mr. Daniel J. Crowe, Indiana State Division of Addiction Services, who will discuss Industrial Alcoholism.

2. Following the presentation, there will be a question and answer session. At the conclusion of the question and answer session, there will be a "Happy Hour" in the Ballroom to afford everyone an opportunity to meet Mr. Crowe.

3. All officers, NCO's in grades E8 and E9, and interested civilians of ADMINCEN and FBH resident commands are invited and encouraged to attend.

FOR THE CHIEF OF STAFF:

H. M. SCHOENBERG
Captain, GS
Asst Chief of Staff

DISTRIBUTION:
1A
6A

CF:
FBH Officers' Club

DEPARTMENT OF THE AIR FORCE
O.L.—A.MALCOLM GROW USAF MEDICAL CENTER (MAC)
BOLLING AIR FORCE BASE, D.C. 20332

REPLY TO
ATTN OF: SGHFB

24 Jul 79

SUBJECT: Temporary Shaving Waiver

TO: Commander *174 MAW DET 1*

1. MOORE DONNISE _____ has been recommended by a
physician for a shaving waiver effective the above date.

2. AF Form 422, "Physical Profile Serial Report," is being processed
and will be forwarded to your organization.

3. This letter does not constitute approval of the waiver by the
commander, but is only evidence that an AF Form 422 is being processed.

4. This letter expires ten (10) days after issue.

DAVID R. RICHMOND, LtCol, USAF, MC
Director, Base Medical Service

GLOBAL IN MISSION — PROFESSIONAL IN ACTION

Internal Revenue Service
memorandum

date: MAR 1 5 1979

to: ~~All Group Managers~~ *AgENTs*

from: Chief, Examination Branch   CP:OIO:65

---

subject: Information Requests

Recently an employee received and apparently answered a telephonic request for information.

Calls from taxpayers for Information Requests should be referred to the Freedom of Information Reading Room at National Office.

Please bring this to the attention of all your employees.

Internal Revenue Service
memorandum

date: May 1, 1979

to: ▓▓▓▓▓▓▓▓ E.O. Specialist
thru
Incentive Awards Coordinator

from: Chief, Office Services Section, Facilities Management Branch

subject: Evaluation of Suggestion 42-EP/EO 132

On April 18 - 19 1978 an Envelope Task Force meeting was held in the
National Office to completely review the Envelope Program. Included
in the review is the types and locations of windows in envelopes. The
target date for completion is the Fourth Quarter FY 79.

Since the National Office had already initiated action in the area of
your suggestion, we can not approve your suggestion.

Thank you for your interest in improving the Envelope Program and for
participation in the Incentive Awards Program.

H. Low

Letters from Your Bureaucrat

(From the computerized letter file of
Senator Dale Bumpers.)

```
ITEM #:     1 ( )
    late apology; fi subj; genrl


     TOP/SUBTOP (1): opening/sorry fi
     TYPE OF DOC.:  opening
     CREATE DATE:  NOV-21-79
     UPDATE DATE:  NOV-21-79
     AIDE:  MP
```

Thank you for contacting me and for giving me your views on
$$subject of letter(.)$$ It is helpful to me to have the benefit
of your thinking, and I hope you will accept my apologies for my
late reply.

```
ITEM #:     2 ( )
    late apology to friend; put aside and pers; ltr


     TOP/SUBTOP (1): opening/sorry informal
     TYPE OF DOC.:  opening
     CREATE DATE:  NOV-21-79
     UPDATE DATE:  NOV-21-79
     AIDE:  MP
```

It was good to hear from you, and I hope you'll accept my
apologies for my delay in getting back to you. I had put your
letter aside to answer personally and time simply got away from
me.

```
ITEM #:     3 ( )
    late apol; put aside to ans pers; fi subj; ltr


     TOP/SUBTOP (1): opening/sorry fi
     TYPE OF DOC.:  opening
     CREATE DATE:  NOV-21-79
     UPDATE DATE:  NOV-21-79
     AIDE:  MP
```

Please accept my apologies for my late response to your letter
regarding $$subject of letter.$$ I had put your letter aside to
answer personally when I was able to give it the time and
attention it deserved, and I was distressed when I realized you
were still waiting for an answer.

Form DOT F 1320.5 (1-67)

UNITED STATES GOVERNMENT

Memorandum

DEPARTMENT OF TRANSPORTATION

OFFICE OF THE SECRETARY

DATE: April 18, 1977

SUBJECT: Correspondence Change for Secretary
Brock Adams' Signature

In reply
refer to: S-10

FROM : Linda L. Smith
Executive Secretary

TO : Executive Secretaries
Correspondence Expediters

Because the Secretary has enlarged his signature, we are asking that a minimum of eight spaces be allowed between the complimentary closing and the typed name of Brock Adams on all correspondence prepared for the Secretary's signature. Please refer to the sample below:

Sincerely,

8 spaces between

Brock Adams

This procedure is effective immediately. I would ask that you alert all of the drafting offices within your agency to this change.

In addition I have found that some letters arriving in the Executive Secretariat are typed on the wrong letterhead stationery, with the inside address exceeding the five line limitation and without proper envelopes. Please see that this is corrected. It would also be appreciated if letters addressed to Congressmen and Senators include the room number on the envelope. (See sample below.)

Honorable Harrison A. Williams, Jr.
United States Senate
Washington, D. C. 20510

Russell Bldg. - 352

Memorandum

TO: Correspondence Unit Chiefs

U.S. DEPARTMENT OF
HOUSING AND URBAN DEVELOPMENT

DATE: May 11, 1981

IN REPLY REFER TO:

FROM: Janet Hale, Executive Secretariat

SUBJECT: Secretary's Style Preferences

In general, Secretary Pierce is quite pleased with the correspondence which has been prepared by the program areas for his signature. Except for instances in which changes of circumstances have created the need to rewrite letters, there have been very few letters sent back to the program areas for rewrite once they have gone through the Executive Secretariat.

The Secretary has very few specific style preferences, other than keeping responses as brief and to-the-point as possible. He does not want to make any commitments which cannot be kept, such as references to a specific time at which a follow-up reply will be made when there is the possibility that this date will not be met. Also, he does not like to encourage further correspondence when it is not necessary, such as by using the closing phrase, "If there is anything else we can do for you, please let us know."

As noted before, his preferred complimentary close is "Very sincerely yours." However, in the event that the response is to a letter from the President, the complimentary close "Respectfully" should be used.

MEMORANDUM

THE WHITE HOUSE

WASHINGTON

February 16, 1979

FOR: WHITE HOUSE ADMINISTRATIVE CONTACTS

FROM: LANDON KITE L K

SUBJECT: Steps to Improve the Quality of
                Presidential Signature Letters

There have been comments concerning the inconsistency in the
quality of letters produced in various offices for President
Carter's signature. On the basis of our discussion with the
representatives of IBM, we offer the following information
for those individuals in your office who type Presidential
signature letters.

There are some steps you can take to eliminate "spatter" on
Presidential letters produced on an IBM Selectric typewriter.
"Spatter" is the tiny extraneous specks of ink and/or little
fuzzy specks around the edges of the individual type-characters.

From a technical standpoint, the harder the impact of the
type ball the more chance there is of "spatter" occurring.
There are two control levers on the IBM Correcting Selectric
typewriter which can be used to reduce spatter. These are:

- COPY CONTROL LEVER

    The copy control lever (located at the left top rear
    section of the typewriter) has five settings, "A"
    through "E", controlling the angle at which the
    type ball meets the paper. The "A" setting is to
    be used for a single sheet of paper and the "E"
    setting is to be used when there are several
    carbons required. It will be necessary for you
    to experiment with your machine to determine the
    best setting for conditions in-between these
    two extremes. The incorrect setting of the copy
    control lever can result in excessive inking or
    spatter.

- IMPRESSION CONTROL LEVER

    The impression control lever (located immediately
    to the right of the type ball) is numbered 1, 3
    and 5 but there are actually five individual

settings available with this lever. Setting "1"
is for a light impact by the ball (when typing
without carbons), and setting "5" is for the
hardest impact by the ball (when producing
correspondence requiring multiple copies). The
harder the impact of the ball, the more chance
there is of ink spattering off the ribbon onto
the paper. The manufacturer of the Selectric
typewriter recommends that the control lever
should be set no higher than "3".

While these two levers can be used to control the quality
of the type produced, there is some variation from machine
to machine. Consequently, you will have to experiment to
get the "feel" of your machine. For example, in order to
type an original only, the lightest settings would be
"A" on the copy control lever and "1" on the impression
control lever. In another situation, where several carbon
copies are required, the settings to the other extreme
could be "E" for multiple carbon copies on the copy control
lever and "5" on the impression control lever for the
hardest impact.

Obviously, experimentation and experience with these control
levers will enable you to produce the best quality of which
your machine is capable. Should you still experience a
problem with "spatter" or fuzziness, even though you are
using the suggested settings for your machine, call the
Office of Administration Supply Office, x2622, and inform
them that you have an IBM Selectric typewriter and are
having problems with "spatter" or fuzziness. There are
additional adjustments that may be required on your Selectric
typewriter. As a result of your call, the service representative will come and do this for you.

We have tried, and will continue to experiment with, different
types and brands of typewriter ribbons but to date, the IBM
Correctable film ribbon yields the best results.

If you have any further questions or comments, don't hesitate
to call me.

Educational Arts Association
National Headquarters

August 15, 1975

Department of Health, Education,
  and Welfare
Office of Education
Office of Business Management
Grants & Procurement Division
School Systems & Handicapped Branch
ROB/3, Room 5914
400 Maryland Avenue SW
Washington, D.C. 20202

   ATTN: C. A. Blum

Dear Sir:

Please send me RFP 76-4.

Thank you.

Sincerely,

Elsom Eldridge, Jr.
Director

M E M O R A N D U M

College of Business Administration and Economics

February 20, 1974

TO: B A & Econ Faculty

FROM: Bryce J. Brisbin, Dean *BJB*

SUBJECT: Physical Change in Classrooms

It has just been brought to my attention that some person or persons unknown have rearranged the tables and chairs in GU 301, our seminar room into a typical classroom arrangement. I don't know the reason for the change but I would remind all faculty that no physical change in a classroom is to be made without the recommendation of the Faculty Advisory Council (see <u>Minutes</u> F.A.C. November 6, 1973, Item No. 1). A change of the seating arrangement in mid-semester without approval of the F.A.C. or the Dean certainly is not in harmony with the F.A.C. statement and might cause serious inconvenience to other users of the room.

In the event any faculty member desires another seating arrangement or other physical changes to the room, please bring it to me in advance and I will refer it to the Faculty Advisory Council for its study and recommendation.

I am uncertain as to what action to take at this time. According to the F.A.C. rule the room should be rearranged into seminar fashion. However, I will await action by the F.A.C. before having the change effected. I would be happy to discuss the room arrangement with any faculty who teach in Guthrie 301.

BJB:hj

DEPARTMENT OF THE ARMY
HEADQUARTERS, 94TH US ARMY RESERVE COMMAND
ARMED FORCES RESERVE CENTER
HANSCOM AFB, MASSACHUSETTS 01731

94th ARCOM Pamphlet   19 November 1979
No. 310-1-1

Military Publications
PREPARATION OF THE ALL PURPOSE FORM

1. PURPOSE. This pamphlet represents the prescribing directive for use of
the 94th USARCOM Form 1, General Purpose Form.

2. GENERAL. The General Purpose Form will be used in lieu of hand sketched
forms used as journals or accountability ledger sheets. The General Purpose
Form may be designed to conform to specific uses by inserting appropriate
titles and ruled lines.

3. RESPONSIBILITY. The DCSPA, 94th USARCOM, will maintain the source of
supply of 94th USARCOM Form 1 and will make additional distribution of forms
to requesting agencies.

(AFKA-ACD-PA)

FOR THE COMMANDER:

OFFICIAL: HENRY P. BELTRAMINI
                                               Colonel, GS, USAR
                                               Chief of Staff

PETER I. CASSELL
Major, AGC, USAR
Adjutant General

1 Incl
94th USARCOM Form 1

DISTRIBUTION: (DL 1-79)
A

GENERAL PURPOSE FORM

94TH USARCOM Form 1, 1 Oct 79
(USARCOM PAM 310-1-1)

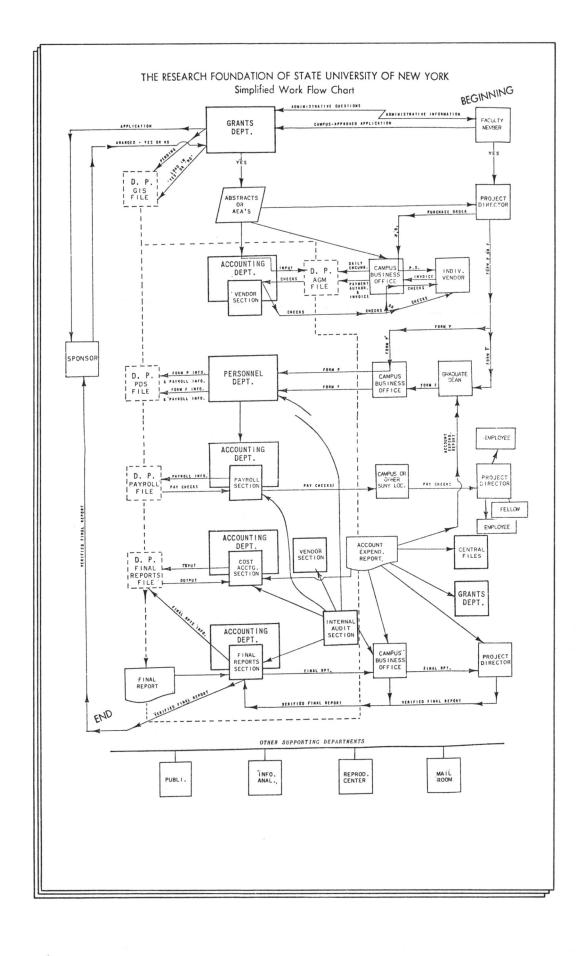

THE RESEARCH FOUNDATION OF STATE UNIVERSITY OF NEW YORK
Simplified Work Flow Chart

ASSOCIATE DIRECTORATE FOR PROGRAMS –
PLANNING AND GUIDANCE STAFF (PGM/G)

Effective immediately PGM/G will be structured as follows:

PGM/G – Planning and Guidance Staff
PGM/GF – Fast Guidance Unit
PGM/GFN – Information Officer, USUN

PGM/G is designated the Planning and Guidance Staff of the
Associate Directorate for Programs. PGM/GF is designated the
Fast Guidance Unit.

The designations Policy Staffs, Issues and Plans Staff and
Fast Policy Guidance Staff and the symbol PGM/GP will no
longer be used.

The position Chief, Issues and Plans Staff is abolished.
The Chief of PGM/G, Mr. Richard Roth, will directly supervise
the members of that former staff, whose functions and
responsibilities remain essentially unchanged.

The International Communication Policy Staff (PGM/C) will
continue as a separate entity, reporting directly to the
Associate Director for Programs.

DISTRIBUTION:　B – Overseas Supervisory Level
　　　　　　　　Y – Domestic Supervisory Level

STAFF ANNOUNCEMENT

UNITED STATES MISSION - BOGOTA

No.	Subject	Date
78	Chargé's New Meeting Schedule	May 29, 1979

References

TO: All American Employees - All Agencies

FROM: Frank M. Ravndal, Administrative Counselor

The following schedule of weekly meetings will remain in effect until the Ambassador returns in mid-July:

1. The 9:30 a.m. Monday Staff Meeting has been cancelled.

2. A short Staff Meeting will be held every Monday, Wednesday and Friday at 9:00 a.m. in the Ambassador's office for those who normally attend the Tuesday, Wednesday and Thursday 9:00 a.m. meetings.

3. The Military Meeting will be held every Tuesday at 9:00 a.m. instead of every Thursday. The Narcotics Meeting will remain the same - every Tuesday at 9:30 a.m.

4. The Country Team Meeting will be held every Thursday at 9:00 a.m. (instead of Fridays) in the Fourth Floor Conference Room.

DISTRIBUTION "D"

The Bureaucrat Clarifies

MEMORANDUM

DEPARTMENT OF HEALTH, EDUCATION, AND WELFARE
SOCIAL SECURITY ADMINISTRATION

TO   :   All Executive Staff   DATE: February 8, 1980

                                                   REFER TO: SAX

                    HRD
FROM   :   Herbert R. Doggette, Jr.
         Deputy Commissioner (Operations)

SUBJECT: Program Misuse and Management Inefficiency--INFORMATION

      In a recent meeting, Secretary Harris informed us that
      in the future, rather than using the phrase, "fraud,
      abuse, and waste," she would prefer "program misuse
      and management inefficiency." I agree that the
      Secretary's terminology more accurately reflects what
      we are measuring and working to eliminate. The change
      is effective immediately; please see that is is
      effected in your areas of responsibility.

      cc:
      OC
      OGC

      OC # 0393

U.S. Department of Labor   Office of the Assistant Secretary
for Administration and Management
230 South Dearborn Street
Chicago, Illinois 60604

Reply to the Attention of: 5APS

OASAM NOTICE NO. 81-59

SUBJECT: NOTICE OF ADVANCE FILE OPPORTUNITIES FOR
U. S. DEPARTMENT OF LABOR EMPLOYEES

DATE: MAY 1 9 1981

TO: ALL EMPLOYEES

1. PURPOSE: To distribute to all U. S. Department of Labor employees
    a list of all entry level bargaining unit positions that are to be
    filled within the Department in the next six months.

2. BACKGROUND: To comply with our agreement of August 17, 1978, with
    the National Council of Field Labor Locals, we are to distribute a
    list of all entry level positions which may be filled within the next
    six months so that interested employees may file advance applications.

3. SCOPE: Due to current hiring and budget restriction, no entry level
    positions are expected to be filled within the next six months.

4. EXPIRATION DATE: October 30, 1981

ROBERT J. UUR
Regional Personnel Officer

NATIONAL AERONAUTICS AND SPACE ADMINISTRATION
WASHINGTON, D.C. 20546

MAR 7 1977

MEMORANDUM

TO: F/Assistant Administrator 3/8
          for Public Affairs

FROM: L/Associate Administrator
          for External Affairs

SUBJECT: Space Shuttle

It has come to my attention that in some documents the
Space Shuttle has been referred to as an "aircraft."

State laws prohibit land overflight of aircraft at
supersonic speeds. Since the Shuttle will carry commercial
cargo at some time, some persons at GAO believe that we
cannot overflight land on entry. This would, of course,
mean the Shuttle could not come down on the KSC Shuttle
Strip.

Consequently, would you please make sure that our Public
Affairs Offices involved refer to it as the "Shuttle" or
"spacecraft" and never as "aircraft."

Herbert J. Rowe

The Washington Post

TO ___THE TEACHER___   FROM ___SCHOOL SERVICES___

RE: SCHOOL SERVICE SCHEDULE

    Due to unforseeable labor problems this department has been unable to operate in accordance with the normal production schedule. One of the pamphlets that was scheduled for this school year, "Work: The American Ethic," will not be printed until next fall.

Bulletin No. 752- 8

Washington, D. C. 20415
February 20, 1979

SUBJECT: Revocation of Supplement 752-1, Adverse Actions
by Agencies

Heads of Departments and Independent Establishments:

Effective January 11, 1979, coincident with the issuance of interim Part 752, Supplement 752-1 became obsolete. Interim Part 752 currently expresses OPM policy on adverse actions and contains all statutory and regulatory requirements implementing chapter 75 of title 5. FPM Chapter 752, which will be issued at the time the interim regulation is replaced by a permanent Part 752, will include guidance and information regarding adverse actions but no additional requirements. Agencies, however, may wish to consider the desirability of placing some of the provisions found in Supplement 752-1 in their own regulations.

Jule Sugarman

Jule M. Sugarman
Deputy Director

Inquiries: Workforce Effectiveness and Development, OPM 632-5623

Code: 752- Adverse Actions by Agencies

Distribution: FPM Supplement 752-1

Bulletin Expires: April 20, 1979

OPM FORM 654   1/79

OFFICE OF THE ASSISTANT SECRETARY OF DEFENSE

WASHINGTON, D. C. 20301

MANPOWER,
RESERVE AFFAIRS
AND LOGISTICS

JUN 6 1977

MEMORANDUM FOR ASSISTANT SECRETARY OF THE ARMY
(Installations and Logistics)

SUBJECT: Standard Transportation Operational Personal Property
System (STOPPS)

In response to our letter of 11 February, Commander, MTMC, on
13 May submitted for approval a list of key developmental milestones
for subject system. Those milestones are approved.

As a related matter, it is apparent that the acronym "STOPPS" can
engender a negative subliminal connotation because of its similarity to
the word "stop." Therefore, in order to reflect the positive approach
of the current effort, the use of the term STOPPS is discontinued and the
program is henceforth to be referred to as the Transportation Operational
Personal Property Standard System with the acronym "TOPS." It is
not desired that previous documentation be changed to reflect the new
terminology. However, future correspondence and documentation should
refer to the developing system as indicated herein.

(Signed) Paul H. Riley
Deputy Assistant Secretary of Defense
(Supply, Maintenance & Services)

Copy to:
ASN (MRA&L)
ASAF (I&L)
ASA (FM)
ASN (FM)
ASAF (FM)
CDR, MTMC

1795-77

DISPOSITION FORM

For use of this form, see AR 340-15, the proponent agency is TAGCEN.

REFERENCE OR OFFICE SYMBOL	SUBJECT
DRXST-OC	Use of the Slash (/) in FSTC Publications

TO DISTRIBUTION "A"	FROM Deputy Director	CMT 1

1. The use of the slash (/) in FSTC publications--to include letters, messages, trip reports, studies, and other forms of written communications--has become so prolific that, in most instances, the reader is unable to understand exactly what the writer is attempting to say. When questioned, the writer usually will state that the intent is for the slash to be interpreted as permitting the use of either of the two words connected by the slash, or both; however, there are many instances where this liberal interpretation makes no sense, i.e., the interpretation must be limited to either and or or. The problem is only compounded when a sentence contains three words connected by two slashes, thereby permitting seven possibilities.

2. Research into this subject reveals nothing that explains the use of the slash as discussed above. One publication indicated that the slash (/) could be used (1) in certain abbreviations, such as B/L for bill of lading (this is not in agreement with AR 310-50, however, which specifies BL for bill of lading); (2) to indicate division, such as 4/5 or 40 cm/s; or (3) in the expression and/or, indicating that the words may be used interchangeably. No interpretation could be found for the use of the slash in the sentence, "The system contained radar/manual/optical controls."

3. To avoid misinterpretation in our writing (to include all forms of written communications), the use of the slash (sometimes called a diagonal or virgule) will henceforth be restricted to its use that indicates division or in the expression and/or where the writer intends to provide the reader with three options as in the sentence, "Robert and/or James will go." This sentence means that Robert may go, that James may go, or that Robert and James may go.

4. Supervisors will see that this restriction on the use of the slash receives the widest dissemination within FSTC and that the restriction is understood and adhered to by all personnel.

JOHN A. ORD
Deputy Director

DA FORM 2496
1 FEB 62

REPLACES DD FORM 96, WHICH IS OBSOLETE.

☆ GPO-1975-665-422/1063

PRESS
DEPARTMENT OF STATE

February 24, 1976

No. 93

REMARKS BY
THE HONORABLE HENRY A. KISSINGER
SECRETARY OF STATE
UPON DEPARTURE FROM
RIO DE JANEIRO, BRAZIL
FEBRUARY 22, 1976

<u>REPORTER</u>: Mr. Kissinger, please say goodbye to the Brazilian people.

<u>SECRETARY KISSINGER</u>: Well, I want to say how much I enjoyed my stay here and how very fond I am of the Brazilian people: its marvelously spontaneous and human people. I hope to be back soon.

<u>REPORTER</u>: Thank you.

<u>SECRETARY KISSINGER</u>: Goodbye.

* * * *

UNITED STATES DEPARTMENT OF COMMERCE
The Assistant Secretary for Administration
Washington, D.C. 20230

MEMORANDUM FOR   HEADS OF ALL OPERATING UNITS

    SUBJECT: Gender-free Terminology

In my prior memorandum on this subject dated August 14, 1978, I recommended that the 1977 Dictionary of Occupational Titles be the reference source for checking sex-specific job titles. I used as an example the terms *stevedore* and *longshoreman*, and stated in a footnote that since *longshoreman* did not appear in the Dictionary, *stevedore* should be used in its stead.

It has come to my attention that, contrary to the contention of the authors of the Dictionary, *stevedore* and *longshoreman* are not the same job.1/ Therefore, please advise your employees that the term *longshoreman* may be used when necessary to interpret the provisions of a statute. Othewise, *longshore worker* is the preferred gender-free term.

It remains the policy of the Department of Commerce to replace gender-specific terms with non-sexist language whenever possible. Our intent is to use gender-free job titles where alternative titles exist, not to alter the substance of jobs. Although the 1977 Dictionary of Occupational Titles appears to have erred with respect to this particular job, it shall remain the general reference for checking job titles.

Elsa A. Porter
Assistant Secretary
 for Administration

1/ A *stevedore* is an employer who is responsible for the loading and unloading of ships. A *longshoreman* is an employee (of the stevedore) who actually loads and unloads ships. The International Longshore Association informs us that its female workers are called "longshoremen."

RECEIVED
4/17/79

SIXTEENTH ANNUAL REPORT

OF THE

TEMPORARY COMMISSION OF INVESTIGATION
OF THE STATE OF NEW YORK

TO

THE GOVERNOR AND THE LEGISLATURE

OF THE

STATE OF NEW YORK

SEPTEMBER 1974

MEMORANDUM

TO: Staff

FROM: Bill Hayes *BH*

SUBJECT: Timesheets

DATE: March 21, 1980

Final timesheets for the month of March are due by noon Monday March 24th.

JAMES A. PREVOST, M.D., Commissioner

Support Division
JOHN URBAN, Deputy Commissioner
Bureau of Capital Operations
GERALD CLAY, Director

April 23, 1981

TO: Steve DeSorbo   Ira Rubenstein
           Jack Bellick   George Roberts
           Don McGuire   Dan Duffy
           Steve Zoltan   Gene Pezdek
           Jack Carey

FROM: Jerry Clay

SUBJECT: Time Management

     Jack Carey recently completed a time management course
and has appropriately stated that certain times of the day must be
"meeting free" if work is to be accomplished. I (and by copy of this,
Steve and Ira) will (unless for a "real" crisis) not be scheduling
meetings during weekdays between 9:00-10:00 and 1:30-2:30.

     An attempt should be made by "all" staff to keep these
times open for actual work. I would appreciate feedback on this at
staff meetings in a few weeks.

FEDERAL TRADE COMMISSION
WASHINGTON. D. C. 20580

May 2, 1980

NOTICE TO THE STAFF

FROM: Director, Data Processing and
Information Systems Division

SUBJECT: Weekly Activity Report (WAR)

The FTC staff spent the entire day of May 1st, 1980 preparing for an orderly cessation of agency activities. To reflect accurately on work-force utilization in CPTS/WAR, it is requested that the WAR hours for May 1st be reported in the following manner:

1. Activity Code 00 is to be used in reporting these hours. This activity code is newly created, and is denoted "Orderly Cessation of Agency Operations".

2. These hours should be charged to "W" programs (i.e., W11, W16). For organizations that do not have "W" programs, no program code should be used.

3. Hours should not be charged to projects or cases.

4. Leave should be charged to Activity Code 17 in accordance with regular procedures.

Please check with your organizations' WAR coordinator or the CPTS/WAR Systems Manager (202-523-3367) if you have any questions regarding this notice.

Anthony T. Green

Distribution: All Employees
(Headquarters and Regions)

MEMORANDUM

DEPARTMENT OF HEALTH, EDUCATION, AND WELFARE
SOCIAL SECURITY ADMINISTRATION

TO : Mr. Louis Zawatzky

DATE : January 4, 1974

REFER TO: IAD 245

FROM : Frank G. Matejik

SUBJECT: Highlight Report for the Week Ending January 4, 1974

<u>ITEMS RECOMMENDED FOR THE COMMISSIONER</u>

None

<u>ITEMS FOR THE ASSISTANT COMMISSIONER</u>

IV. Continuing activities:

   1. Negative

Gary E Good
for Frank G. Matejik

UNITED STATES GOVERNMENT

Memorandum

DEPARTMENT OF HEALTH, EDUCATION, AND WELFARE
REGION IV — ATLANTA

TO : Title IX team (Unit II)

DATE: November 18, 1977

FROM : Carroll D. Payne
Coordinator, Title IX team

REFER TO:

SUBJECT: Routing of completed drafts of Title IX reports and letters.

The above drafts come to me first for review and I then give them to
Mr. Gregory for typing. The typist returns them to Mr. Gregory for
his record of typing completions. Mr. Gregory will return the typed
copies to the originator to review for typing corrections and/or
sign off. The originator, after corrections and sign off, will route
the typed report or letter to me for sign off and routing to Mr. Clements.
Copies of mailed letters come back through Mr. Gregory for recording.

HELP ELIMINATE WASTE   COST REDUCTION PROGRAM

GPO : 1968 O—797-836

DEPARTMENT OF DEFENSE
WASHINGTON HEADQUARTERS SERVICES
WASHINGTON, D. C. 20301

5 NOV 1979

MEMORANDUM FOR SECRETARIES OF THE MILITARY DEPARTMENTS
　　　　　　　　CHAIRMAN OF THE JOINT CHIEFS OF STAFF
　　　　　　　　UNDER SECRETARIES OF DEFENSE
　　　　　　　　ASSISTANT SECRETARIES OF DEFENSE
　　　　　　　　GENERAL COUNSEL
　　　　　　　　ADVISOR TO THE SECRETARY AND DEPUTY SECRETARY
　　　　　　　　　　OF DEFENSE FOR NATO AFFAIRS
　　　　　　　　ASSISTANTS TO THE SECRETARY OF DEFENSE
　　　　　　　　DIRECTORS OF THE DEFENSE AGENCIES

SUBJECT:　Conversion by the Department of Defense of Federal
　　　　　　Government Stationery from 8 by 10.5 inches to
　　　　　　8.5 by 11 inches

The Administrator of General Services, by Temporary Regulation B-5, dated
September 21, 1979, copy attached, has advised Federal Agencies of
procedures for conversion of stationery from 8 by 10.5 inches to 8.5 by
11 inches.

The purpose of this memorandum is to issue guidance with respect to
stationery size for correspondence forwarded to the Secretary or Deputy
Secretary of Defense for either information or decision.

In consonance with Paragraph 5 of the basic attachment, DoD components
may continue to use 8 by 10.5 inch stationery until stocks are depleted
with the proviso that all pages of correspondence, inclusive of attachments
thereto, forwarded to the Secretary or Deputy Secretary of Defense will be
of uniform size. The provisions of Paragraph 1. c., Attachment A to
Temporary Regulation B-5, which authorizes intermixing of stationery sizes
are not applicable for correspondence to be forwarded to the Secretary and
Deputy Secretary of Defense.

D. O. Cooke
Director

Attachment

CONVERSION PROCEDURES

1. <u>Correspondence management practices.</u>

a. Use all existing stocks of 8- by 10.5-inch stationery including letterhead, plain bond papers, manifold carbon tissue sets, and carbon paper.

b. Do not redistribute 8-inch-wide stationery stock if redistribution costs exceed the purchase-and-distribution costs for new 8.5-inch-wide stock.

c. In preparing correspondence, intermix stationery sizes if that is the only method that will deplete 8- by 10.5-inch stock. However, when using 8.5- by 11-inch bond papers with 8- by 10.5-inch carbon sets, use at least .75-inch side margins.

d. When printing or procuring 8.5- by 7.33-inch stationery, the 7.33-inch length should not vary more than .05 inches.

2. <u>Mail management practices.</u> Ensure that the size of self-addressed, return envelopes can accommodate the size of the document(s) to be returned.

3. <u>Directives management practices.</u> When issuing a page change for a directives system using lettersize paper, consider the following:

a. If the revisions involve changing 50 percent or more pages, issue the entire directive in an 8.5- by 11-inch format;

b. If there is less than 50 percent revision, allow a single directive to stay intermixed; and

c. If a directive of four or fewer sheets is revised, reprint the entire directive on 8.5- by 11-inch paper.

4. <u>Forms management practices.</u>

a. Consider using 8.5- by 11-inch paper for new or revised forms that are commonly interfiled with correspondence. However, use existing stocks of 8- by 10.5-inch forms before converting.

b. All other form sizes should be determined according to the use of the individual form.

5. <u>Copy management practices.</u>

a. Consider using 8.5- by 11-inch copy stock instead of 8- by 10.5-inch stock.

b. When copying an entire document containing both 8- by 10.5-inch and 8.5- by 11-inch paper, use the 8.5- by 11-inch size.

6. <u>Word processing practices.</u> For 8-inch-wide paper, some word processors have a preset margin that limits line length to 6 inches. Readjust the preset margin to extend line length to 6.5 inches for use with 8.5- by 11-inch paper.

ASSISTANT
ADMINISTRATOR

OCT 2 3 1979

Mr. Ray Kline
Deputy Administrator
General Services Administration
18th and F Streets, N.W.
Washington, D.C. 20405

Dear Mr. Kline:

The Agency For International Development has encountered a problem
of some proportion which I bring directly to your attention as it
will soon obtain in all Executive agencies and doubtless generate
costs and embarrassment for the Government if not avoided.

We have found that the new, larger (8½" x 11") standard stationery
prescribed by the Joint Congressional Committee on Printing which
GSA is stocking for Government-wide use beginning January 1, 1980
is too large to fit the stationery drawers of many standard GSA
desks. We discovered that earlier this month when we printed new
letterhead necessitated by a recent reorganization, and converted
to the larger stationery at the same time to avoid costs of a second
conversion three months later.

We have found no single, easy solution of the problem but, rather,
have been improvising -- exchanging desks for others in stock,
providing desk-top holders and employing other costly devices.

Perhaps the Federal Supply Service can with this advance note of
the general problem find some central way to avoid it for the
Government as a whole.

                              Sincerely,

                              D. G. MacDonald
                              Bureau for Program and
                              Management Services

cc: Mr. Boulay, GSA

Date: July 2, 1981

To: AA/OPC

From: Administrator

Subject: SBA Stationery

I have decided that I want the Agency to continue using the stationery
with the seal which it has been using until exhausted. Then, I
want the Agency to use the new stationery with the SBA logo until it
is exhausted. At that time, we will again use the stationery with the
seal. No additional stationery with the logo is to be purchased.

Please take the necessary actions to ensure that the stationery with the
seal is released for use until exhausted and that additional stationery
is ordered when needed.

Michael Cardenas

Interdepartment Message

STO 201 REV 7-78   STATE OF CONNECTICUT
(Stock No. 6938-051-01)

SAVE TIME: *Handwritten messages are acceptable.*
Use carbon if you really need a copy. If typewritten, ignore faint lines.

To	NAME SEE BELOW	TITLE	DATE APRIL 15, 1980
	AGENCY CORRECTION	ADDRESS	

From	NAME T. DeRIEMER	TITLE MEMBER, STATEWIDE PAPER-	TELEPHONE 5606
	AGENCY	ADDRESS WORK TASK FORCE	

SUBJECT   FORMS COLLECTION

By 1979 Public Act, and DAS Commissioner Memo, the State Purchasing
Division is required to gather <u>ALL</u> forms in use by <u>EVERY</u> State Agency
and sub-unit.

We are providing a cover sheet to attach to each format in use by your
unit (Reproduce additional copies locally, if needed). Your collected and
labeled forms should be forwarded to me <u>no later than April 30, 1980</u>. Only
clean, unused forms should be submitted.

Any obsolete forms which you discover in this process should be contributed
to paper recycling efforts. Negotiable or numerically-controlled form sets
(such as gas coupons or traffic tickets) should not be provided in original
form unless voided. Submit photo copies instead.

<u>HERE ARE THE RULES</u>:

1. <u>Collect</u> three copies of <u>every</u> form used by your unit. Paper-clip the
   group of three. To the <u>top copy</u> of each group, affix a "Forms Use Report.

2. <u>Complete</u> the "Forms Use Report" for each forms group.

3. <u>Sort</u> the forms into 15 piles by FORM CLASS--I.A.

4. <u>Sort</u> each of these groups <u>by size of form</u> to make handling easier.

5. <u>Separate</u> the forms which have been assigned a form number (e.g. CO-17,
   STC-93, HCSP-201) from those which have no assigned number.

6. FUNCTIONALIZING: For FORM CLASSES (I.A.) 1 thru 5, <u>only</u>, identify the
   ACTIVITY (Table II) and FUNCTIONAL VERB (Table III) which most specificall
   identifies the agency activity which is responsible for ultimately using
   the data on the form and what action the completed form envisions.

EXAMPLES OF FUNCTIONAL CODING

		ACTIVITY	FUNCTION
A.	CO-17 Vendor Invoice		
	Function: REQUESTS Payment from Accounts Payable		
		1.5 Accounts Payable	.08 Request
★ B.	SP-10 Purchase Requisition		
	Function: REQUESTS Purchase of Commodity or Service by Bur. of Purch.		
		9.6 Purchasing	.08 Request
C.	CO-94 Purchase Order		
	Function: ORDERS Commodity or Service through Purchase		
		9.6 Purchasing	.05 Order

SAVE TIME: *If convenient, handwrite reply to sender on this same sheet.*

7. A. When the function coding is completed, wrap or box all forms in CLASS CODES 1-5 by FUNCTION .01 thru .08 (Table III) and send to Correction Central Office, Attn: T. DeRiemer.

   B. Wrap or box the sorted CLASS CODES 6 - 15 for delivery to the Correction Central Office, Attn: T. DeRiemer. This group is not to be sorted beyond the requirements of Step 3.

Forms Collections will be required from:

        Office of Commissioner
        Deputy Commissioners
        Facility Administrators
        Division Chiefs
        Board of Parole
        Board of Pardons

Continued

FORMS USE REPORT

TO: T. DeRIEMER, DOC Central Office (Agency # 8001)
340 Capitol Ave., Hartford, CT 06106

FROM (Name): _____ DIVISION: _____ ACCT #: _____
(Note: Data on above line should specify the origination point of this form)
ATTACHED ARE 3 COPIES OF THE SUBJECT FORM IN USE BY THIS DIVISION:

FORM NAME: _____
FORM   DATE OF LATEST   NO. OF THIS FORM
NO.: _____   REVISION: ____/____/____ USED ANNUALLY: _____
IS THIS FORM EVER REQUIRED FROM A MEMBER OF THE BUSINESS COMMUNITY, OR
IS IT COMPLETED OR REVIEWED BY PRIVATE, NON-AGENCY PEOPLE? ___(Y); ___(N)

I.A. FORM CLASS (Circle the code which best describes)

These forms will require FUNCTIONALIZATION using Table III, below.	NOTE: Divisions are not required to to classify these CLASSES by funtion.

I.A CLASS DESCRIPTION
CODES

1 SHEETS, LOOSE	6 FORM LETTERS	11 TAGS
2 SHEETS, PADDED	7 LETTER HEADS	12 LABELS
3 SHEETS, IN SETS	8 INTER-OFFICE MEMOS	13 ENVELOPES
4 SNAP-OUTS	9 CHECKS	14 BOOKS
5 CONTINUOUS	10 CARDS	15 MISC.

Within all CLASSES, forms are to be grouped by size and form no., e.g.:
SIZE A   SIZE B   SIZE C

1) Numbered forms, in order:
2) Un-Numbered forms:

I.B. SOURCE (Circle the code which indicates how your forms were produced)

I.B SOURCE
CODES   DESCRIPTION

I IN-HOUSE PRINTING	F FURNISHED BY OTHER STATE OR FEDERAL AGENCIES, OR FIRMS WITH WHOM THE STATE DOES BUSINESS (EG. INSURANCE FORMS).
P PURCHASES	
O CENTRAL WAREHOUSE	
C COPY MACHINE	

II. ACTIVITY AREA CODE (Circle the primary use code)

1.1 General/Cost Acctg	3.1 Executive	9.1 Engineering
1.2 Payroll	3.3 Office Services	9.2 Production
1.4 Credit & A/R	3.7 Legal	9.3 Shpg & Recv'g
1.5 A/P		9.6 Purchasing
1.6 Systems & Data Proc	7.0 Marketing & Sales	9.4 Warehousing
1.8 Audit, Tax & Ins		
1.9 Order Proc & Cust Serv		12.0 Personnel

III. PRIMARY FUNCTION (Circle the code and explain the Function)

CODE	EXPLAIN	CODE	EXPLAIN
.01 ACKNOWLEDGE _____		.05 ORDER _____	
.02 ADVISE _____		.06 RECORD _____	
.03 AUTHOR _____		.07 REPORT _____	
.04 INSTRUCT _____		.08 REQUEST _____	

Table III-A
VOCABULARY FOR FUNCTIONAL FILE
Secondary Functional-Verbs

A

Accept .01
Account for .06
Acknowledge .01
Adjust .03
Admit .03
Admonish .04
Advise .02
Agree .01
Allot .03
Analyze .07
Apply for .08
Appoint .03
Appropriate .03
Approve .03
Arrest .05
Arraign .06
Assign .05
Audit .07
Authorize .03

B

Bill .08
Budget .08

C

Cancel .05
Catalogue .06
Certify .01
Change .05
Charge .08
Claim .08
Clarify .02
Code .06
Collect .08
Commend .01
Complain .07
Compute .06
Confirm .03
Confiscate .05
Consent .01
Contract .03
Control .05
Credit .02

D

Deliver .05
Dispose .05
Distribute .05
Document .07
Dun .08

E

Encumber .05
Enforce .05
Estimate .06
Evaluate .07
Examine .07
Exempt .03
Extract .08

F

File .06
Fingerprint .06
Follow-up .08

I

Identify .06
Indict .06
Index .06
Inform .02
Inquire .08
Inspect .07
Instruct .04
Interview .06
Introduce .02
Inventory .07
Investigate .07
Issue .05

J

Justify .03

L

Label .06
License .03
List .06

M

Move .03

N

Notify .02

O

Offer .02
Order .05

P

Pay .03
Permit .03
Petition .08
Plan .06
Prescribe .05
Produce .05
Purchase .05

Q

Qualify .03
Question .08

R

Rate .07
Receipt .01
Record .06
Refer .04
Refuse .03
Register .06
Reimburse .03
Release .03
Remove .05
Renew .05
Reply .02
Reprimand .04
Report .07
Request .08
Requisition .08
Return .03
Review .07
Route .04

S

Salvage .05
Schedule .05
Sell .03
State .02
Stop .05
Sue .08
Summarize .07
Summon .05
Supplement .03
Swear .01

T

Tag .06
Test .07
Transact .05
Transfer .05
Transmit .03

U

Update .07

V

Verify .01

W

Waive .03
Warn .02

*M*emo From the Desk of

MARCY BYRD
Secretary of the Senate

Arizona State Senate

January 24, 1979

TO: ALL SENATE PERSONNEL

RE: Committee Minutes - Blue C.O.W.Calendar

This is to alert you that due to the unavailability of blue paper, the committee minutes and blue committee of the whole calendars will be xeroxed on white paper.

MARCY BYRD

NINETY-FIFTH CONGRESS

ED JONES, TENN., CHAIRMAN
JOHN H. DENT, PA.   WILLIAM L. DICKINSON, ALA.
MENDEL J. DAVIS, S.C.
JIM ABERNATHY, CLERK
225-4568

COMMITTEE ON HOUSE ADMINISTRATION
FRANK THOMPSON, JR., CHAIRMAN

Congress of the United States

House of Representatives

COMMITTEE ON HOUSE ADMINISTRATION

SUBCOMMITTEE ON SERVICES

105 CANNON HOUSE OFFICE BUILDING

Washington, D.C. 20515

September 1, 1978

Dear House Employee:

I am happy to report the success of the first month of "specials" offered by the House Beauty Shoppe. The Subcommittee on Services maintains oversight of this operation and in conjunction with the management of the Shoppe will offer another month of price reductions in September.

September will bring the fall season and the House Beauty Shoppe will present DISCO DAZE. Every Tuesday and Wednesday, special prices will be in effect for service on hairstyles, hair coloring, and permanents. Free nail decals will be given with each manicure or pedicure at the regular price. Full details on all the specials are available by calling 225-4008.

Hours of operation are from 7:00 a.m. to 4:30 p.m., Monday through Saturday. Service is provided for Members of Congress, staff, and the general public. The House Beauty Shoppe is located in the Cannon Building, room 139, just off the main rotunda.

I hope you will be able to take advantage of the excellent service, outstanding expertise, and the September "DISCO DAZE" specials.

With kindest regards and best wishes, I am

Sincerely,

Ed Jones
Chairman

RICHARD H. ICHORD
8TH DISTRICT, MISSOURI

2302 RAYBURN HOUSE
OFFICE BUILDING
TELEPHONE: (202) 225-5155

COMMITTEES:
ARMED SERVICES

SUBCOMMITTEE:
CHAIRMAN, RESEARCH AND DEVELOPMENT

SMALL BUSINESS

Congress of the United States
House of Representatives
Washington, D.C. 20515

DISTRICT OFFICES:
HOUSTON:
116 MAIN STREET
TELEPHONE: (417) 967-2270

JEFFERSON CITY:
P.O. BOX 298
TELEPHONE: (314) 634-3810

RE: Physical Exercise
    Self-Defense
    Mental Discipline

Dear Colleague:

For your physical and mental self-improvement, I am happy to announce the formation of the U. S. Congressional Martial Arts (Tae Kwon Do, Karate, Kung Fu) Club. I have been a member of the Club from the time it was organized in 1972 and am confident you will find the Karate Training stimulating and beneficial both physically and mentally.

My good friend Jhoon Rhee, who is one of the world's most renowned experts (Nobody Bothers Him) has again volunteered to teach the class. Classes will be held in the House Gymnasium one day a week at a time which you members select as the most convenient and will begin the fourth week in March.

Some of you might remember the Democratic vs. Republican Karate competition held at the D. C. Armory in 1975. The event was covered by ABC, CBS and NBC television as well as U.P., A.P. Parade and other magazines. We plan another such event this year for those members of the class who wish to compete. Competition, however, is not required to attend the class exercises.

If you are interested in attending the class, please fill out the enclosed card and return to me promptly. I am sure you will find the Martial Arts training to be a great program for physical conditioning and mental discipline as well as an inspiration to others to participate more in physical activities. There is no age limit. You should, however, be alive and kicking. Just return the card and report to the gymnasium when we advise you and we will get you back into condition if your physical condition is deficient.

Dick

Richard H. Ichord, President
U. S. Congressional Martial Arts Club

P.S. Past members are Bevill, Spence, Roybal, Fauntroy Gradison, et al.

JON HINSON
4TH DISTRICT, MISSISSIPPI

COMMITTEES:
BANKING, FINANCE AND
URBAN AFFAIRS
EDUCATION AND LABOR

Congress of the United States
House of Representatives
Washington, D.C. 20515

MARSHALL HANBURY
ADMINISTRATIVE ASSISTANT

1312 LONGWORTH BUILDING
WASHINGTON, D.C. 20515
(202) 225-5865

DISTRICT OFFICE:
FEDERAL BUILDING
ROOM 222
P.O. BOX 22662
JACKSON, MISSISSIPPI 39205
(601) 969-3300

MEMORANDUM
April 30, 1980

TO: Congressman Hinson
        All Staff Members
FROM: Marshall
RE: Payment/Coffee--Main Office

Since we have an obvious problem with our system of payment for coffee in the main office, we have come up with a new system.

The "regular coffee drinkers" and average number of cups each day seems to be as follows:

Hinson	2 cups
Marshall	5 cups
Ruthie	5 cups
Jennifer	4 cups
Constituents	2 cups
Spillover	2 cups
TOTAL	20 cups-average each day

The former system of payment involved 15 cents per cup, which the person was supposed to put in the box each time he got a cup. However, due to lack of time, etc., these regular payments were not made.

Therefore, after office discussion, we decided that a flat weekly payment for each regular coffee drinker would be a more feasible way to handle this matter. Figured at 15 cents per cup, the amount charged to each regular coffee drinker would be the following.

Hinson	$4.50
Marshall	$3.75
Ruthie	$3.75
Jennifer	$3.00

This payment should be made to Virginia on Monday morning of each week, at which time you will be checked off. (The payments may be made in lump if desired.)

Please note that this "kitty" will cover the following: coffee, cream, sugar, and dishwashing liquid.

If a staff member other than the "regular coffee drinkers" wishes to have a cup of coffee, he should pay 20 cents to Virginia for that cup.

Let's try this system for a while and see how it works. If everyone cooperates, we should be able to eliminate those old problems, such as no funds to buy coffee. See Virginia or myself with comments or suggestions.
vjs

CONFIDENTIAL

The markings on this page (the
last page of this report) represent
the OVERALL security classification
assigned to this report. By itself
this page is UNCLASSIFIED.

CONFIDENTIAL